Nurses
Help Us

Aaron R. Murray

Enslow Elementary

an imprint of

Enslow Publishers, Inc.

40 Industrial Road
Box 398
Berkeley Heights, NJ 07922
USA

http://www.enslow.com

Enslow Elementary, an imprint of Enslow Publishers, Inc.
Enslow Elementary® is a registered trademark of Enslow Publishers, Inc.

Library of Congress Cataloging-in-Publication Data
Murray, Aaron R.
  Nurses help us / Aaron R. Murray.
    p. cm. — (All about community helpers)
  Summary: "Introduces pre-readers to simple concepts about what nurses do using short sentences and
repetition of words"—Provided by publisher.
  Includes index.
  ISBN 978-0-7660-4044-1
  1. Nursing—Juvenile literature. 2. Nurses—Juvenile literature. I. Title.
  RT61.5.M867 2013
  610.73—dc23
                                        2011031047

Future editions:
Paperback ISBN 978-1-4644-0056-8
ePUB ISBN 978-1-4645-0963-6
PDF ISBN 978-1-4646-0963-3

Printed in the United States of America
032012 Lake Book Manufacturing, Inc., Melrose Park, IL
10 9 8 7 6 5 4 3 2 1

To Our Readers: We have done our best to make sure all Internet Addresses in this book were active
and appropriate when we went to press. However, the author and the publisher have no control over and
assume no liability for the material available on those Internet sites or on other Web sites they may link
to. Any comments or suggestions can be sent by e-mail to comments@enslow.com or to the address on
the back cover.

♻ Enslow Publishers, Inc., is committed to printing our books on recycled paper. The paper in every
book contains 10% to 30% post-consumer waste (PCW). The cover board on the outside of each book
contains 100% PCW. Our goal is to do our part to help young people and the environment too!

Photo Credits: © 2011 Photos.com, a division of Getty Images, pp. 1, 12–13, 22;
iStockphoto.com: © Imgorthand, pp. 14–15, © Michael Booth, p. 6; Shutterstock.com,
pp. 3, 4, 8–9, 10, 16, 18–19, 20.

Cover Photo: Shutterstock.com

Note to Parents and Teachers

Help pre-readers get a jump start on reading. These lively stories introduce simple concepts with
repetition of words and short simple sentences. Photos and illustrations fill the pages with color and
effectively enhance the text. Free Educator Guides are available for this series at www.enslow.com.
Search for the *All About Community Helpers* series name.

Contents

Words to Know

hospital **medicine** **temperature**

Nurses take care
of people.

Nurses go to school
to learn how to take
care of people.

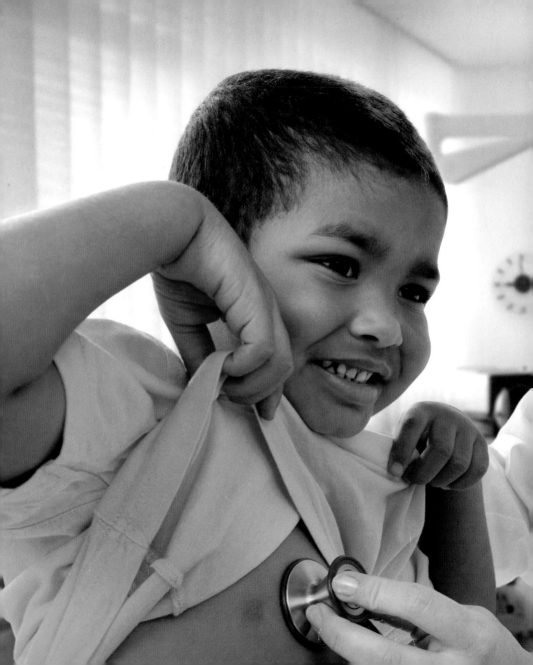

**Nurses listen
to your heart.**

Nurses take your
temperature.

Nurses check your eyes.

13

Nurses check your ears.

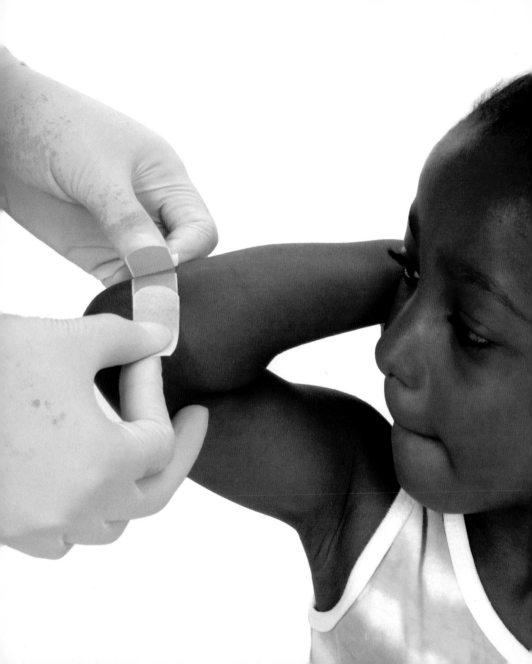

Nurses help you feel better.

Some nurses work in schools. You see the nurse when you feel sick.

Some nurses work
in hospitals.

They help
the doctors.

Do you like taking care of people?

You may want to be a nurse.

Read More

Kenney, Karen Latchana. *Nurses at Work*. Mankato, Minn.: Magic Wagon, 2009.

Morris, Ann. *That's Our Nurse*. Minneapolis, Minn.: Millbrook Press, 2003.

Schaefer, Lola M. *We Need Nurses*. Mankato, Minn.: Capstone Press, 2006.

Web Sites

KidsHealth: For Kids
<http://kidshealth.org/kid/index.jsp?tracking=K_Home>

NIEHS: Kids' Pages
<http://kids.niehs.nih.gov/>

Index

Guided Reading Level: C
Guided Reading Leveling System is based on the guidelines recommended by Fountas and Pinnell.

Word Count: 75